"A much-needed encouragement for orthodox Christians across the worl[...] s to be faithful to C[...] on. A call to follow [...] and truth. A must re[...]



[...]nda

"A timely resource for faithful believers to address the increasingly sensitive issue that the global church is facing: the gender revolution. This book is a powerful reminder that we are all preachers of the message of reconciliation to bring all sinners to Christ. Soli deo gloria."

**Jaehoon Lee, Onnuri Church; Korean Lausanne Committee**

"Wise, hopeful and Christ-honouring, this book will be of great comfort and practical help to those beguiled or betrayed by the lies of the sexual revolution, and those who walk alongside them as disciples of Christ."

**Archbishop Kanishka Raffel, Australia**

"For Christians seeking a way forward that is true to Scripture and the way of Christ, this is an excellent introduction to key issues in the LGBTQ discussion. It is theologically reflective, pastorally sensitive and relevant cross-culturally. I commend it wholeheartedly."

**Bishop Hwa Yung, The Methodist Church, Malaysia**

"This book is about more than sex and sexuality; it invites us to delight in God's beautiful design and find ultimate satisfaction in Christ. I recommend this book to Christians of all backgrounds."

**Rev Dr Patrick Fung, OMF International**

"Vaughan Roberts speaks not only with theological conviction of the authority of Scripture but also with authentic credibility as one who is openly resolved to submit his own sexuality to the lordship of Christ. Grace and truth also shine through his pastoral heart for those whose struggles are compounded by loneliness and a crushing lack of understanding in churches. May they find comfort and courage in these pages."

**Chris Wright, Langham Partnership**

"A marvelous book for 'such a time as this!' Our generation is starving for this conversation. I believe Vaughan Roberts is the best voice on this crucial topic. He speaks to real people from life experience, bringing the truth of Scripture in an incredibly compassionate way."

**Sarah Breuel, Founder, Revive Europe**

"A wonderful pastoral, biblical, and deeply human guide to one of the most complex issues of our time. With great courage, clarity, and yet profound compassion, *Full of Grace and Truth* offers a vision that is faithful to Scripture while remaining sensitive to the real struggles that many people face in the Church today regarding this topic."

**Archbishop Enrique J. Lago, Chile**

"This book meets the crying need for a biblically grounded, bold, compassionate and holy response to the sexual revolution. It gives clear guidance and hope to those seeking to be faithful to God but faced with a confusing array of voices calling for their attention."

**Ajith Fernando, Youth for Christ, Sri Lanka**

"Questions about human sexuality and gender are not only matters of frequent public controversy, but are often matters of deeply personal and hidden struggle. In this helpful book, Vaughan Roberts charts a path forward as he shares his own testimony of following Christ amidst temptations and struggles."

**Bishop Paul Donison, General Secretary, Gafcon**

"Vaughan Roberts is a much-respected leader of immense courage and integrity. He has faithfully taught and pastored one of the largest churches in Oxford for 27 years. He addresses complex and challenging issues with the authentic voice of vulnerability and sensitivity."

**Nicky Gumbel, Founder, Alpha International**

"A call to countercultural Christian sexuality. It is a challenge to faithfully preach a biblical sexual ethic while offering grace, compassion and hope to those who falter. It is also a call to all Christians, to live a life in keeping with God's good design for sex and gender even when it clashes with the convictions of our sexualised permissive culture."

**Patricia Weerakoon, author, *The Gender Revolution***

# FULL OF GRACE AND TRUTH

VAUGHAN ROBERTS

# FULL OF GRACE AND TRUTH

The gospel and sexuality in the global church

10 Publishing
a division of 10 of those.com

First published in Great Britain in 2026



British Library Cataloguing in Publication Data
A record for this book is available from the British Library

EU GPSR: 6b Upper Water Street, Newry, BT34 1DJ

ISBN: 978-1-83728-155-8

Cover design and typeset by Jude May
Cover image © Yolandi Outram | iStock

Printed in Denmark

10Publishing, a division of 10ofthose.com
Unit C, Tomlinson Road, Leyland, Lancashire, PR25 2DY

info@10ofthose.com
www.10ofthose.com

1 3 5 7 10 8 6 4 2

# Contents

# Foreword

Sex and human sexuality are things we hardly talk about openly in my African context. Years ago, it was taboo, especially for young people, to utter any word related to these topics or even to ask questions at home, at school or in church. Hence silence or secret whispers were the norm. The HIV and AIDs pandemic awakened us out of that mindset, but questions remained as to how to respond to ever-changing sexual revolution and realities, not only in western contexts but at our very doorsteps. How do we, as followers of Jesus, remain faithful to biblical truth and at the same time exercise grace towards others on these matters? Beyond silence on the one hand and strict legislation on the other – be it within church or by governments – boundaries between grace and truth remain blurred in our response.

In this short book, rightly called *Full of Grace and Truth: The Gospel and Sexuality in the Global Church,* Vaughan has done remarkably well in providing sound biblically balanced guidance on rather complex issues. How the gospel relates to human sexuality and various responses and attitudes towards others has made the subject such a "hot potato" that many prefer to be silent on. In addressing this subject, Vaughan has affirmed that Scripture must be the interpreter of culture, perspectives and preferences. Given the silence or even the fear of speaking openly about this within the church, this book is a timely resource for more deliberate reflection, teaching and conversation on how Scripture must guide our response and attitude, especially towards others, not as either being full of grace *or* truth, but with both grace *and* truth in our relationships and witness.

With the aim of providing "an accessible starting point for readers who want an introduction to the Bible's perspective on sexuality", Vaughan has, on the one hand, not shied away from addressing liberal tendencies that tend to marginalise biblical truth in the name of grace to accommodate almost any or all views of human sexuality. On the other hand, he has not shied away from addressing tendencies of conservatives who, in commitment to biblical truth, affirm or impose strict Christian morality, especially towards others, to the point of legislation or stereotyping.

I find the stories he has included helpful to illustrate how difficult or challenging the journey has been, and continues to be, for many people. Regardless of our context or experience, I commend this book to us wholeheartedly, not least because Vaughan's call for us to delight in God's design for human sexuality, to be humble and compassionate, as well as to embrace Christ's revolution, is essential for the times we live in. I wish all churches and fellowship groups would use this book and the discussion questions included as a resource for study and conversation.

*Femi B. Adeleye*
*Institute for Christian Impact*
*Ghana,*
*July 2025*

# Introduction

In 2024, I was asked to speak at the Fourth Lausanne Congress in South Korea. Since its foundation under the leadership of Billy Graham and John Stott, the Lausanne Movement has convened four great global conferences: in Lausanne (1974), Manila (1988), Cape Town (2010) and Seoul (2024). It was a privilege to stand before over 5,000 evangelical leaders from 202 countries, but it was also hugely daunting, not least because of the subject I had been given: "Identity and Sexuality".[1]

There is surely no more sensitive topic than sexuality. It is, of course, deeply personal. We all bring our own emotions and experiences to any treatment of the subject and, however careful a speaker is, it is inevitable that some raw nerves will be touched. The subject is also highly contentious. The sexual revolution of recent decades has led to a rejection of traditional understandings of morality throughout the West and, increasingly, all over the world, especially in younger generations. This in turn has resulted in conflict between traditionalists and progressives, both in society as a whole and within churches. But the conflict goes wider still: it is also seen among those who are united in holding firmly to the Bible's teaching on sex and marriage, as it has always been understood by Christians down the ages, and yet have very different instincts about how to uphold, express and apply this doctrine pastorally, apologetically and politically within the church and the world.

## A cross-cultural approach

These differences of perspective, which exist within every individual Christian culture, become more pronounced in cross-cultural settings, as was very evident at the Congress in Seoul. The paragraphs on sexuality, sex and marriage in the statement, which was published in advance of the gathering, were condemned for being both too conservative and too liberal. On the day of my address, local Christian protesters held banners outside the convention centre urging delegates to "shout out to LGBTQ to repent", while others inside were lamenting what they felt was a weakening of the pastoral tone of the statement, after changes had been made in response to criticism.[2]

Given this background, you can imagine my trepidation as I pondered what to say. The challenge was made harder by the strict time limit I had been given for the talk of just 15 minutes. It seemed like an impossible task as, over a period of weeks, I produced and rejected draft after draft. What could I possibly say that gave the appropriate challenge and encouragement for everyone present, given the huge range of cultural contexts represented? And how could I make a useful contribution to such an important and sensitive topic in so short a time? But as the preparation process continued, I came to believe that these constraints, although challenging, brought some significant benefits.

The central section of this book contains my address in Seoul, almost exactly as I gave it. I hope its brevity will make it an accessible starting point for readers who want an introduction to the

Bible's perspective on sexuality, as well as helping those who are very familiar with this territory to refocus on the essential principles.

Most treatments of this subject have a specific cultural context in view which inevitably, and rightly, governs the selection and presentation of the material. I am well aware that we can never be completely free of our particular cultural glasses, and I certainly do not claim to have achieved this but, with the help of friends from very different cultural contexts to mine, I have sought to expound and apply the Bible's teaching to a global audience.

My experiences, both within the Lausanne Movement and the global Anglican Church, to which I belong, have convinced me of the great value of a cross-cultural approach. Our personalities and cultural backgrounds, in varied Christian communities and wider societies, give each of us different perspectives and instincts, which can both help and hinder our responses to issues of sexuality. We are often quick to see the blind spots of others, without recognising our own. Conversation with Christians from other cultural contexts, who share our commitment to biblical orthodoxy and yet have some very different perspectives to ours, can be mutually beneficial in providing much needed encouragement and challenge.

## Precious people

My primary ministry is as a pastor. As I prepared to speak at the Lausanne Congress, I had in the forefront of my mind those who have opened up to me about their personal struggles. Too often their experiences have revealed significant failings in churches across the world which, far from helping, have only added to their burdens. I had wanted to put some of their stories in my address, but time constraints prevented me. By including them here, I hope to remind us that any discussion of sexuality has a huge impact on the lives of countless precious people such as these. I have changed their names and some minor details to preserve anonymity.

Joseph had been looking at pornography since his early teens. He knew it was wrong and tried to stop, but never managed for long. Over the years he had often thought he should talk to someone at church, but shame held him back. Everyone else seemed so godly that he could not imagine any of them would understand, so he kept quiet.

It was only after his wife saw some images on his phone that he was forced to speak to a friend at church. By that time his sin had become so deeply entrenched that it was very hard to address. It could have been so different if the culture in the church had made it easier for him to talk earlier.

Naomi is a young woman who had recently come to Christian faith. When she discovered I was a pastor, she began to enquire about my views on various issues. "What about sex and sexuality?" she asked. When I told her I believed the Bible taught that the place for sex was within the marriage of a man and a woman, she said, almost under her breath as if she was admitting a dangerous secret, "I think that too." She then told me that she was fairly sure the pastors in her church also had the same understanding, but she was not certain, as they never taught on these issues. "They don't want to put anyone off from coming to Christ, or cause division in the church, so they keep quiet," she said. The result was, she told me, that the members of the church, who were mostly young, were just confused. They received no guidance from their leaders on one of the most significant areas they were all having to grapple with.

Phoebe was visibly shaking as she told me of her experience of same-sex attraction. She had not shared this with anyone before, so it was a huge moment for her. Such matters were never mentioned in her culture, except in strong denunciations of the sins of the godless. It did not occur to her pastor that any true Christian could experience a struggle in this area. Phoebe was seeking to live a godly life, but her isolation made the challenge so much harder. "I feel so lonely," she said. She lives in Africa, but I have heard many similar stories from all over the world, including in conservative western contexts.

Kate was crying as she described how her family had been torn apart. Unbeknown to her mother or siblings, her father had been struggling for many years with the desire to dress and present as a woman. When he had shared this with his pastor, he had received nothing but affirmation and encouragement to embrace his "true self". Soon afterwards, to the great distress of his wife and children, he adopted a female name and identity. Through her tears, Kate said, "I have lost my dad."

Jethro had never wanted to tell anyone about his struggles with sexuality, least of all any member of his church, but the sense of shame and guilt became unbearable, so he blurted something out to his youth leader. Days later, the senior pastor called Jethro to a meeting and told him that if he truly trusted in the Lord, he would be delivered. The pastor then prayed over him, claiming God's power to release him from the oppression of demons. That was it. There was no attempt to listen to him and understand his experience; no word of encouragement; no follow up whatsoever. The conversation was never referred to again. Jethro felt more desperate than before, not least because he experienced no change to his desires and temptations.

I could tell countless similar stories. Many church leaders have been intimidated by changes in cultural attitudes into adapting their teaching or staying silent, so as not to cause offence. Others have held firmly to the Bible's teaching, but have failed to connect pastorally with the real lives of many in their congregations and in the world. Because shame prevents many Christians being open and honest, often pastors lack understanding of the struggles of those in their congregation. This lack of connection is heightened by differences between generations, with younger people being shaped from an early age by what they experience online as much as by the traditional attitudes of their homes and churches.

It is urgent that we help one another across the global church to learn how to respond appropriately to the sexual revolution which continues to sweep across the world. This will help us better serve everyone, both Christians and non-Christians. For some of us the chief challenge is to grow in pastoral understanding and sensitivity. For others, it is to hold firmly to God's truth and resist false teaching. It was with this dual challenge in mind that I stepped onto the platform to give my address at the Lausanne Congress.

# The Gospel and Sexuality in the Global Church

I recently walked into the centre of Oxford, England, where I live, and saw rainbow flags flying wherever I looked: above the Town Hall, university buildings, and even some churches. Those flags, flying high above the city to celebrate LGBTQ+ History Month, were a powerful symbol of the victory of the sexual revolution.[3] That revolution began as a counter-cultural movement in the 1960s, but has now become so mainstream that hardly anyone in public life in my country dares raise questions about its assumptions, for fear of being cancelled. In just a few decades, traditional

Christian teaching about sex and sexuality, which used to be regarded as good and moral, is now thought to be harmful and immoral. In Tim Keller's language, it is one of the chief "defeater beliefs", which makes Christian faith completely implausible to many people.

How should we respond? That is an urgent question, not just for Christians in the West but for the global church. Be in no doubt that the message of the sexual revolution has already spread rapidly throughout the world, via technology, and has captured the hearts of many in your country, wherever you live, especially young people. So if we are to reach them for Christ, keep them in our churches and build them up to mature discipleship, we must *all* engage with this topic.

Our response should not be limited to a few isolated texts, but must rather reflect deeply on the whole of biblical theology and especially on its three essential themes of Creation, Fall and Redemption.

## CREATION: We must delight in God's design

God's design for sex and marriage appears in the opening chapters of Genesis and is affirmed throughout Scripture. It can be summarised in a few simple statements:

GOD'S DESIGN FOR SEX AND MARRIAGE

- God is for sex
- Sex is for marriage
- Marriage is for life

### *God is for sex*

> *"So God created mankind in his own image, in the image of God he created them; male and female he created them." (Gen. 1:27)*

Sex is a good part of God's Creation. He made us as physical sexual beings. We are not just humans who happen to have male or female reproductive organs. Our sex is fundamental to who we are created to be in God's image: "male and female he created them".

### *Sex is for marriage*

> *"... a man leaves his father and mother and is united to his wife, and they become one flesh." (Gen. 2:24)*

Having created our complementary sexuality (male and female), God instituted marriage as the proper context for its sexual expression. Genesis 2:24 is the Bible's definition of marriage, endorsed and quoted by the Lord Jesus and the apostle Paul in the New Testament (Mt. 19:5; Eph. 5:31). Sex is designed to express, seal and strengthen the "one flesh" union of one man and one woman. It is in the context of that union that God intended children to be conceived, born and raised.

### *Marriage is for life*

> *"Therefore, what God has joined together, let no one separate." (Mt. 19:6)*

Jesus said these words after quoting Genesis 2:24. The Bible does make allowance for divorce, but only as a concession, given the mess of life in a fallen world. It was not part of God's original design.

These instructions are here, not because God is a spoil sport, wanting to stop us having fun, but for our good. All the Bible's negative prohibitions in relation to sex are designed to protect the great positive of God's precious gift of marriage for the flourishing of individuals, families and wider society.

This teaching was rejected by the sexual revolution as narrow and oppressive. That revolution is rooted in a profound individualism, which resists restrictions on the right to self-define and live accordingly. This way of thinking is in the cultural air we all breathe. It's in advertising slogans like PlayStation's "Be whatever you want to be"; in songs such as "This Is Me" from *The Greatest Showman*; and in movies where it forms the moral of almost every fairy story, once it has received the Disney treatment. It proclaims that the path to true freedom is to resist any external limitations, whether from traditional morality, religion or even biology, and "be true to yourself". That sounds enticing, but it has not delivered.

Just think of the legacy of the sexual revolution in the western world. The prioritising of self-fulfilment over obligations and feelings above commitment, has led to the undermining of the family unit with devastating consequences for the whole of society, felt disproportionately by the vulnerable, especially children.[4] And the irony is that this path does not even lead to the individual fulfilment it is intended to promote. It has resulted in many lonely, isolated people and has surely contributed to the West's epidemic levels of anxiety among the young. At an age when their hormones are raging and sense of self is unstable, they are being asked to identify their own sexuality and even their gender, regardless of what their bodies proclaim them to be. Twenty-two percent of Gen Z in the US define as LGBTQ+.[5] But it is a desperately insecure identity, based on uncertain feelings.

To the generation less able than any other in history to answer the question, "Who am I?", we can offer stable foundations on which they can build their lives. We can tell them: "You are a man or a woman, made in the image of God, of infinite value and worth." To those who sense the dislocation within themselves and in society, caused by the prioritising of the self, not least in the area of sexuality, we can point to God's better way. We have not been left to ourselves to try to navigate a path through life. God has given us the Maker's instructions, which are for our good.

Are we teaching these truths? Far too often churches say little or nothing about sex and sexuality, leaving their members to be shaped by the counter-message of the world. Others go further and adapt their teaching to fit in with the culture. They say we need to look again at the Bible and interpret it in a way it has never been interpreted before and that goes against the natural reading of the relevant texts. This approach lacks theological and exegetical integrity on a first order issue and is tearing churches apart. It is also missionally ineffective. Revisionist churches are in terminal decline. Why would people come to church to hear an echo of what they already hear in the world? We have nothing to be ashamed of; far from it! We must resist false teaching, but rather *delight in God's design*.

## FALL: We must be humble and compassionate

We turn next to the perspective of the Fall. The delightful scene at the end of Genesis 2, with Adam and Eve both naked and feeling no shame, no longer reflects the reality in a world infected by sin. Our sex and sexuality, designed to result in joyful intimacy, is often experienced, at least in part, as a cause of alienation and pain.

The Bible teaches that "all have sinned" (Rom. 3:23). Sin has corrupted every part of us, including our sexual desires. In one sense, none of us is "straight"; we are all crooked. We may have only ever experienced attraction to the opposite sex, but which of us could say that our desires and actions have always been pure? Jesus taught that "anyone who looks at a woman lustfully has already committed adultery with her in his heart" (Mt. 5:28). We are *all* sexual sinners. That recognition should lead to a deep *humility.*

If we know our own hearts, we dare not look down self-righteously on others, perhaps especially those who identify as LGBTQ+, or shun them, as if any contact with them would somehow defile us. Our Lord Jesus condemned the Pharisees of his day for just such behaviour. There should be absolutely no place in our churches for any stereotyping, demeaning language or attitudes which give others the impression that they are unlovable, unforgivable and unwelcome. Jesus was known as the "friend of sinners" (see Mt. 11:19) who, far from avoiding the sexually broken, reached out to them in love. One of the first converts in Acts was the Ethiopian eunuch who would be described as "gender queer", in the language of some in the West.

As disciples of Christ our first instinct must be to follow his example in reaching out to all with loving friendship and the good news of God's amazing grace, as we marvel at the mercy he has shown to us. Paul teaches in 1 Corinthians 5:12 that it is not for us to judge the world in matters of sexual morality; we should leave that to God. That should surely caution us before we add our voices to calls for criminal sanction in this area, especially when it is only targeted at one type of sexual sin. And while it is surely right to advocate for Christian values in the public sphere, believing them to be good for the flourishing of all society, we should do this with humility, as fellow sinners who have been saved by God's grace. Our most instinctive posture should not be, first and foremost, one of condemnation towards the world, but rather to follow Christ's example in opening out our arms in loving welcome to all.

But, having said that we are not "to judge those outside the church", the apostle does say clearly that we should "judge those inside" (1 Cor. 5:12), by which he means the exercise of church discipline in relation to unrepentant sinful behaviour within the church. Church discipline should be without discrimination. In

1 Corinthians 6:9-10, Paul includes persistent theft, greed, drunkenness, slander and swindling in a list of sins which, without repentance, exclude people from the Kingdom of God. He does also refer to "men who have sex with men", but only having first mentioned "adulterers" and "the sexually immoral" in general. There is no justification for focusing only on some sins, while remaining silent about others.

Will we also call for repentance from pornography, domestic abuse and the abuse of pastoral power, including for sexual gratification, which are far too common in churches and yet rarely addressed? And as we call on others to repent, will we ensure that we search our own hearts and lives and turn from sin ourselves?

An undiscriminating call for repentance must then be matched by an undiscriminating offer of the grace of salvation to all. There is a glorious inclusivity in the gospel message. All have sinned, without exception. All deserve condemnation by the holy, just God. And all, whatever the particular nature of our sins, are invited to receive forgiveness through Christ's blood, so that we too can be among those who are "washed … sanctified … [and] justified in the name of the

Lord Jesus Christ and by the Spirit of our God" (1 Cor. 6:11). This perspective must surely lead, not just to humility, but also *compassion.*

When we speak on matters of sex and gender we must always remember that we are not just talking about "issues", but about precious people, made in God's image and greatly loved by him. We are all impacted by the effects of the Fall in these areas, but some are affected more acutely than others such as, for example, those who experience a disharmony between the sex of their body and how they feel in their psyche. That must be agonising. Others are predominantly or entirely attracted to the same sex. What causes such attractions is debated and will vary from person to person, but there is no doubt that they are not simply chosen and often cause considerable distress.

Such people are not just out there in the world or in the West; they are in your country, in your churches and at this Congress. They are in the room whenever we speak on these topics. Does our content and tone reflect that reality? Many have felt that they dare not speak about their experience for fear that they would be looked down on or even driven away. This has too often resulted in the terrible isolation of loneliness and shame, which only add to the burdens they already feel and make it more likely they will fall into sinful patterns of thinking and action.

It was out of a pastoral concern for others that I began to speak publicly a number of years ago about my own experience of same-sex attraction.[6] I first became aware of it in my early teens and assumed it would disappear, but it never did and, for many years now, I have only been attracted to the same sex. That is not my identity, but it is an ongoing part of my reality. As a Christian I do not think it right to pursue a romantic or sexual relationship with someone of the same sex. I seek to live my life in obedience to Christ by resisting temptation and have remained celibate. It has been challenging to be faithful to Christ in this area, as it is for all of us, whatever our sexual attractions. By speaking openly, I wanted others to know that they were not alone. A few of us set up the Living Out website (www.livingout.org), which has been an encouragement to large numbers throughout the world. They include many of the most godly Christians I know.

Would people like them feel able to open up to others in your church? As a young man experiencing a lonely struggle, I was acutely aware of the tone and language that others used. Sweeping generalisations in favour of, for example, "a hard line against gays", made me feel that it would not be safe to be open with anyone. But I can still remember the impact of a preacher mentioning homosexual feelings, alongside heterosexual temptations, as a reality some in the church would be experiencing and then kindly adding: "If that's you, please don't let it be a lonely battle. Do talk to someone." Those words made an enormous difference to me and gave me the confidence to speak to a pastor for the first time. They provide a great model for us all. In the light of the Fall, we should certainly not change or lower God's standards, but *we must be humble and compassionate.*

## REDEMPTION: We must embrace Christ's revolution

Having considered the perspectives of Creation and the Fall, we now turn to Redemption. Christ's saving work changes everything. By far the greatest revolution in human history began when Christ came to bring salvation and introduce God's Kingdom. That provides the perspective from which we need to respond to the sexual revolution, which is spreading throughout the world today.

And yet, not only revisionists, but too often conservatives as well, have been shaped in our perspectives on matters of sex and sexuality by a truncated view of the impact of Christ's revolution.

Revisionists stress inclusion, but say little about repentance. Christ did indeed say to everyone, "Come as you are!", but he does not say: "Stay as you are!" Conservatives, by contrast, are strong on the importance of repentance and holiness in all areas of life, including sexual behaviour, but we have too often focused only on moral rules and not enough on the relationship which Christ offers to all who come to him, which provides the motivation and power by which we can obey them. This brings us to the vital fourth element in a biblical understanding of sex and marriage. God is for sex, sex is for marriage, marriage is for life but also, most importantly, *life is for Christ*.

GOD'S DESIGN FOR SEX AND MARRIAGE

- God is for sex
- Sex is for marriage
- Marriage is for life
- Life is for Christ

The conviction that life is for Christ changed everything for me. When I became a Christian in my late teens it was not that I was gripped and excited by Christian morality. No! I was gripped and excited by Christ. By the Spirit my eyes had been opened to the beauty of Christ as the way, the truth and the life. I loved him and, loving him, I wanted to live for him.

Human beings are creatures of desire. The seductive message of the sexual revolution, with its promises of freedom and fulfilment, has captured the imagination of a generation. We must respond, not with moralism, but by inspiring hearts with the beautiful story of the gospel, which centres on the person of Christ.

The Bible is a love story. It starts with human beings, made by God to relate to him, turning away from his love. That could have been the end of the story but God, in his amazing grace, will not let us go. He sent his Son on a mission of love, as a bridegroom seeking a bride, who was so committed to wooing and drawing us to himself that he died to make that possible. All who turn to Christ experience a taste of joyful union with him by the Holy Spirit, as we look forward to the day when he returns and we will be fully joined to our divine husband. We will then, at last, enjoy the fullness of the ultimate relationship for which we were made.

When the apostle Paul quotes the words of Genesis 2:24, referring to the one flesh union of marriage, he adds: "This is a profound mystery – but I am talking about Christ and the church" (Eph. 5:32). He is telling us that the fundamental marriage is the union of Christ and his people, of which the union of a man and a woman is a reflection. This truth both exalts and relativises human marriage.

We have too often failed to work out the revolutionary implications of the gospel for our understanding of marriage, singleness and family. Yes, we should certainly value human marriage as a precious gift of God, but we should keep it in its proper perspective. Finding and sustaining a romantic relationship is *not* the key to life. Our sexual and emotional longings express a yearning for union which will never be fully satisfied in any human relationship. If we forget that truth, we will place an impossible burden on our spouse or friend. Above all, we were made to relate to God. Human marriage is only for this life (Mt. 22:30), but our relationship with Christ will last forever.

This perspective will also change our view of singleness, viewed by so much of the Christian world as just a problem to be solved. I even know of one church which called its young adults' group, "Pairs and Spares". Have they never read Matthew 19 or 1 Corinthians 7, which speak of singleness as a positive vocation? Do we ever preach on such passages in our churches? Singleness, whether chosen or not, is a precious gift, which provides extra opportunities for Christ's service.

Single Christians need to be encouraged that they are not alone. We may not experience a sexual, romantic relationship, but that certainly need not, and should not, mean a life without intimacy. The pain of unfulfilled sexual and emotional longings can even be used, in God's kindness, to strengthen our dependence and delight in him. We should also experience the joy of being part of Christ's family, the church.

While the New Testament affirms our responsibilities to our biological families, it also speaks of a new spiritual family to which all Christians belong, as we walk together on the road to glory. We dare not call our fellow disciples to costly discipleship in the area of sex and relationships if we do not at the same time open our hearts, lives and homes to them. There should be no isolated people in the church of God; and yet too often there are.

It made all the difference to me when a family invited me into their home on the same evening every week and made me feel part of the family. My Christian brothers and sisters enhance my life in so many ways, but their greatest gift to me – and mine to them – is to point to Christ, the living Saviour, and encourage joyful dependence on him. He alone can offer the "living water" that can truly satisfy (Jn. 4:10).

So how should we as Christians respond to the sexual revolution? We should respond with Christ: Christ's teaching (he affirmed God's Creation order), Christ's example (he showed amazing love to sinners) and Christ's welcome (he invited all to come to him in repentance and faith).

To a thirsty world, made more thirsty by the failed promises of the sexual revolution, and to thirsty Christians, too often beguiled by those promises and feeling they are missing out, we must come, not with a wagging finger, but with the open, wounded hands of Christ's love and the offer of a deeply satisfying, life-transforming relationship with him. To those cast down by the guilt and shame of sin, not least sexual sin, he offers perfect cleansing through his death. To those experiencing the isolation and pain of a difficult marriage, bereavement or unwanted singleness, he draws especially close.

There will be joys, even in this fallen world – not least of family, friendship and fellowship – but there will be many sorrows too, including the ongoing pain of our broken sexuality. And yet, in the midst of it all, there is the transforming power of the Holy Spirit, who works in and through our pain to draw us closer to Christ. And there is hope, always hope: the glorious knowledge that one day Christ will be fully united to his bride and then, at last, all our wounds will be healed, all our tears wiped away and all our longings fulfilled.

Brothers and sisters, the Bible's teaching about sex and marriage is nothing to be ashamed of, still less to change! Our world is hurting and we have glorious good news to share. Let us preach and live Christ for the glory of his name!

# Afterword

The reaction to my talk at the Lausanne Congress was mixed. There was appreciation from across the world, along with more negative responses. Many liberal Christians in the West believe the traditional understanding I expounded to be both outdated and oppressive. Some Christians from the Majority World continued to believe that the issues I raised were essentially western problems and did not apply to their countries. There were also those who expressed confusion and concern at the reference I made to my own struggles.

However, I continue to hope that my brief words in Seoul will be a catalyst for discussion and, where needed, change across the very different cultural contexts represented by those present.

## Western revisionism

I have never enjoyed conflict, but from very early on in my ministry I felt compelled to join with others in resisting a revisionist trend within my own Anglican Church. The same pressures are felt in many other denominations in the West, and often come to a head over matters of sexuality, especially over whether same-sex partnerships should be blessed. This has led me to speak and write on these topics, and engage in the exhausting business of church politics.[7] In all this I have been driven by the conviction that, at heart, the dispute is not simply about sex, but also about Scripture, sin and salvation.

Will we submit to the authority of the Bible, even if its teaching clashes with the deeply held convictions of our culture? And can we really claim to be faithful to Scripture if our new interpretations clash, both with the natural meaning of individual texts and with the overall trajectory of biblical teaching, as it has always been understood by Christians until very recently? The stakes are high, not least because issues of sexual morality are never regarded in the Bible as secondary matters of conscience, about which Christians can agree to disagree.

They rather concern questions of holiness and sin, from which we are called to repent if we are to be assured of salvation (1 Cor. 6:9-10).

Those who have sought to uphold traditional Christian beliefs and practice have often been accused of being divisive, but it is surely those who have departed from the teaching of the church down the ages, which is still upheld by the vast majority of Christians throughout the world, who are responsible for causing disunity. Speaking of my own denominational context, as the Church of England has been torn apart over these issues, I have been greatly encouraged by the faithfulness and support of fellow Anglicans in Africa, Asia and South America, who greatly outnumber revisionist Anglicans in the West.

There is already external diplomatic and economic pressure on countries in the Majority World to adapt their Christian sexual ethic and this pressure is likely to increase from within as younger generations are influenced by the assumptions of the sexual revolution through the material they access on their phones. It is not just faithfulness to Scripture that requires us to resist this, but also love for people. However attractive it may appear, that revolution has not delivered the individual liberation it promised and has had a devastating impact on western society as a whole.[8]

The first heading of my Lausanne address was intentionally positive: "We must delight in God's design". I longed to remind the global church, represented by those in attendance, of the goodness of God's purposes for sexuality so they might be confident in both proclaiming and upholding them.

## Personal background

For a long time I only spoke of my experience of same-sex attraction with a few close friends, but a number of years ago I decided to be much more open. My motivation in speaking out publicly was chiefly pastoral. When Christians had shared with me about struggles with their own sexuality, I had been struck by how isolated they felt. Whereas, in my cultural context, they were offered many positive models of those who had embraced a gay lifestyle and identity in the world, they often knew of no one else who experienced similar challenges, while seeking to be faithful to biblical teaching. This made them wonder if this path of costly discipleship really was liveable. I met others who had remained entirely silent in Christian circles, for fear of misunderstanding or rejection, before leaving in desperation and finding community elsewhere.

Christians from the Majority World have sometimes been shocked and confused when I have referred to my experience of same-sex attraction. For some it can be hard to see a distinction between attraction and lifestyle. Many have never met an orthodox Christian who has been similarly open and so they have no existing category to put me in. I have even been told by a brother from another continent that "we have no homosexuals in our churches". But what did he mean by "homosexual"? Did he mean someone who identified themselves by their desires and sought to live accordingly? If so, that is certainly not me. My identity is as a child of God, united to Christ and called to live in fellowship with and obedience to him. For me this has meant celibacy. Or did he mean someone who experiences exclusive or predominant same-sex attraction, regardless of lifestyle? I suspect he was not entirely clear himself.

There needs to be a greater openness to talking about issues of sexuality in many cultures. This should help to address misunderstandings and also make it easier for those who are struggling to talk to others. Silence only increases the isolation they already feel and makes it more likely that they will live hidden lives of secret compromise.

While the first section of my Lausanne talk was an appeal to Christians to hold fast to the biblical teaching on sex, the second was designed to prompt discussion about how we can best do that with pastoral sensitivity and grace. What that will look like will no doubt vary from culture to culture, but we will benefit from seeking to learn from one another. While upholding God's design in Creation, we must also recognise the impact of the Fall on each one of us. In our different ways we all have distorted desires, records of past failures and ongoing struggles, not least in the area of sexuality. God has sent his Spirit to help us fight sin and grow in godliness but, although he could, he has not promised to remove our particular battles and temptations. The fight continues. *So we must be humble and compassionate.*

## Full of grace and truth

I have chosen the title *Full of Grace and Truth* for this book. There is surely no Christian who would deny the importance of both grace and truth, and yet there is a tendency for us, individually and in our communities, to be stronger in one or the other in our contribution to discussions about sexuality. We can be suspicious of what we perceive as either the harsh dogmatism or the weak compromises of those whose knees jerk instinctively in the opposite direction to ours, while failing to see any weaknesses in our own approach. Faithfulness to Scripture and the example of Jesus demand a passionate concern for *both* grace *and* truth.

Far from softening the teaching in the Old Testament on sex and marriage, our Lord reaffirmed it and strengthened its application (Mt. 5:17-20, 27-30; Mk. 10:1-9). And yet, instead of shunning those who had failed to live up to this standard, he shocked the self-righteous Pharisees by seeking out sexual sinners and offering them his love and mercy (Jn. 4:1-26; 8:2-11). His teaching and example is a challenge to us all. Surely our chief concern, as we engage in these sensitive matters, must be to stay faithful to him and to long that others would come to know him as their loving bridegroom, who alone can satisfy all the longings of our hearts.

It is for this reason that the most important section of my Lausanne talk is the last. It contains a challenge to us all to fully embrace the impact of the gospel on our perspectives on sexuality. Revisionist Christians have subtracted from the gospel in stressing inclusion, in a way that just echoes the world. But conservative Christians also have their own form of subtraction. Too often we focus on Christian morality, especially in pointing out the sins of others, and not nearly enough on Christ's love. The result, in traditional cultures, can be that we simply confirm our societies in the rightness of their own moral instincts, without bringing the counter-cultural challenge of the gospel. In liberal societies, by contrast, this approach is seen as harsh, judgemental and deeply off-putting. Neither of these is the way of Christ.

## "The new way of the Spirit"

In Romans 7:6, Paul contrasts "the old way of the written code" with "the new way of the Spirit". The old way is moralism: a focus on moral rules. This is not only unfruitful evangelistically; it is also spiritually unproductive, and even harmful, for Christians. It breeds self-righteousness in those who are satisfied that they have kept within the letter of God's law. It also produces hypocrisy: a focus on external conformity to sexual standards, without addressing the heart. Such hypocrisy is almost always accompanied by a deep, underlying shame, despite attempts to suppress it. God's law has the power to condemn, but not to transform. In the marital imagery of Romans 7, a union between God's moral law and a sinful human heart is sterile. It does not produce the fruit of godliness, but rather bears "fruit for death" (Rom. 7:5).

By contrast, "the new way of the Spirit" focuses on proclaiming the gospel of Christ: his amazing grace in dying and rising for sinners, so that anyone, no matter how we have lived, may be freed from condemnation and be united to him. The Holy Spirit not only initiates that union at conversion, but deepens our understanding and delight in being joined to Christ, as he applies the gospel to our hearts through his Word. The result is a fruitful union (Rom. 7:4), which grows in love for Christ and leads in turn to hatred of sin, longing for holiness and compassion for the lost.

I once heard about the parents of a teenage boy, who were concerned about how much time he was spending on online gaming. They tried everything to stop him, issuing repeated stern warnings and severe punishments, but nothing worked. But then, a while later, they noticed that their son was no longer interested in what had previously obsessed him. What do you think had changed? He had met a girl! The games he had so loved before now seemed very dull in comparison with spending time with her.

That story contains a lesson for our engagement as Christians in the world. Too often we have been known for what we are against, but moral denunciations will not draw the world to Christ or enable Christians to live for him. Nor, in isolation, will reminders of God's standards. We should certainly affirm God's design for sex and marriage and, for the good of society, we may feel the need to advocate for marriage laws in accordance with God's design, but we must not stop there. Human marriage is a precious gift, but it was never intended to be ultimate. Above all, we were made for a union with God, which Christ has now made possible. Our privilege as Christians is to point to him as the heavenly bridegroom who invites us all into loving relationship with him. That perspective changes everything. It brings wonderful, life-transforming news for all people everywhere: Christian and non-Christian, African, American, Asian and European, single and married, "gay" and "straight". *We must embrace Christ's revolution.*

# Questions for Discussion

*The impact of the sexual revolution*

- Since the 1960s, the West has experienced a sexual revolution emphasising radical individualism, free sex, and the right to abortion and divorce. What is the impact of this revolution in your country
    - » in society?
    - » among Christians?

*Creation: We must delight in God's design*

- How is God's design for sex and marriage good news for individuals and society?
- What negative effects do you see when it is rejected?
- Are we teaching these principles enough and in the right way? If not, how could we do better?

*Fall: We must be humble and compassionate*

- How do you think Christians are getting it wrong in our attitudes and actions towards others? How should we change?
- Is it right to recognise a difference between desire/inclination and action?
- To what extent do people feel able to share their struggles, including in the areas of

sex and sexuality, in our churches? How could we help one another more?

*Redemption: We must embrace Christ's revolution*

- How should the gospel change our perspective on
    - marriage?
    - singleness?
    - family?
- How does our relationship with Christ help us in our struggles?
- What is the good news we have to offer the world?

# Endnotes

1. The video of this talk can be found here: <lausanne.org/video/restoring-biblical-sexuality>
2. The Seoul Statement can be found here: <lausanne.org/statement/the-seoul-statement>
3. LGBTQ stands for lesbian, gay, bisexual, transgender and queer. The history month is marked in some countries as an opportunity to learn from the experience of sexual minorities in the past and to celebrate their communities in the present.
4. See, for example, Part 2 of Glynn Harrison, *A Better Story: God, Sex & Human Flourishing* (IVP, 2017).
5. Jeffrey M. Jones, "LGBTQ+ Identification in U.S. Now at 7.6%", 13 March 2024, <https://news.gallup.com/poll/611864/lgbtq-identification.aspx>
6. I have spoken about my experience of same-sex attraction in an interview for *Evangelicals Now*: Julian Hardyman, "A Battle I Face", *Evangelicals Now*, 1 Oct 2012.

7. See, for example, Vaughan Roberts, *Together in Love and Faith?: Should the Church Bless Same-sex Partnerships?* (Latimer Trust, 2022), a free download can be found on the publisher's website; Vaughan Roberts and Peter Jensen, *Faith in a Time of Crisis: Standing for the Truth in a Changing World* (Matthias Media, 2017); and Vaughan Roberts, *Transgender* (The Good Book Company, 2016).
8. See, for example, Louise Perry, *The Case Against the Sexual Revolution* (Polity, 2022).